If you were a

MINUTE

by Trisha Speed Shaskan
illustrated by Francesca Carabelli

PICTURE WINDOW BOOKS
Minneapolis, Minnesota

:60 :60 :60 :60 :60 :60 :60 :60 :60

Editors: Christianne Jones and Jill Kalz
Designer: Lori Bye
Page Production: Melissa Kes
Art Director: Nathan Gassman
Editorial Director: Nick Healy
The illustrations in this book were created with acrylics.

Picture Window Books
151 Good Counsel Drive
P.O. Box 669
Mankato, MN 56002-0669
877-845-8392
www.capstonepub.com

Printed in the United States of America in North Mankato,
Minnesota. 042010 005773R

All books published by Picture Window Books
are manufactured with paper containing
at least 10 percent post-consumer waste.

Library of Congress Cataloging-in-Publication Data
Shaskan, Trisha Speed, 1973-
If you were a minute / by Trisha Speed Shaskan ;
illustrated by Francesca Carabelli.
p. cm. — (Math Fun)
Includes index.
ISBN 978-1-4048-5201-3 (library binding)
ISBN 978-1-4048-5202-0 (paperback)
1. Time measurement—Juvenile literature. I. Carabelli,
Francesca. II. Title.
QB209.5.S53 2009
529—dc22
2008037910

Special thanks to our adviser for his expertise:

Stuart Farm, M.Ed., Mathematics Lecturer
University of North Dakota

If you were a minute ...

... you would be a part of everyday life.

It takes Carlos 1 minute to wash his hands.

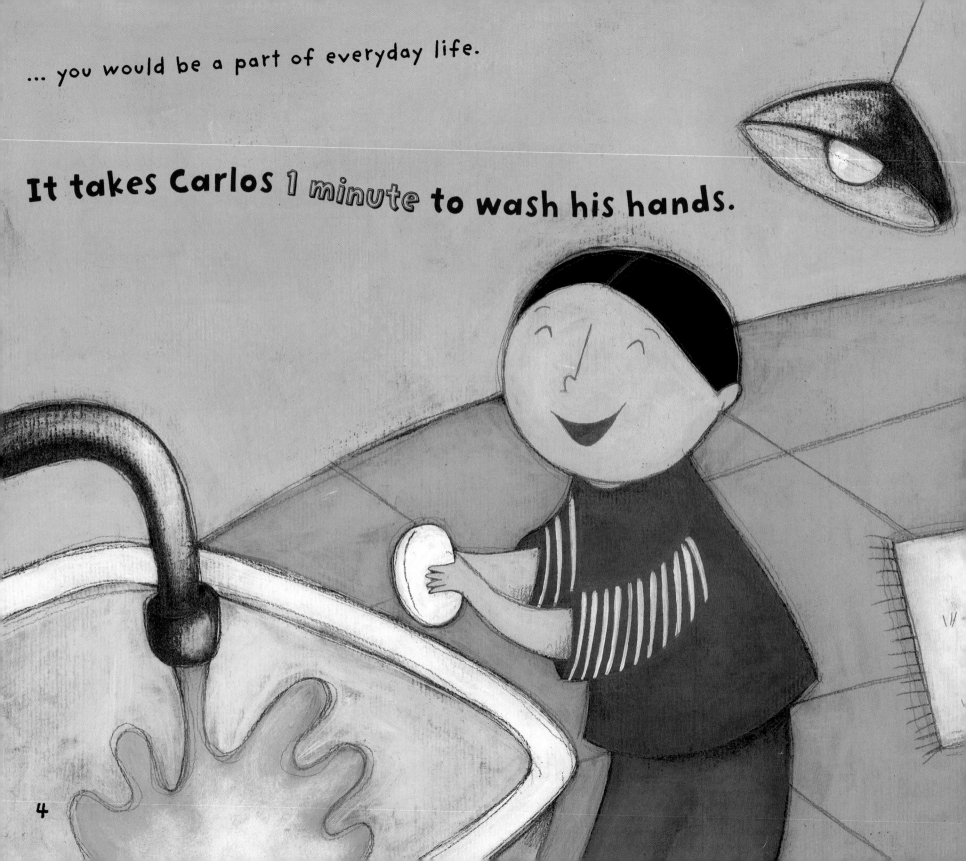

Flora can sing the alphabet three times in 1 minute.

It takes Porter 1 minute to tie his shoes.

If you were a minute, you would measure time. Minutes are made up of seconds. There are 60 seconds in 1 minute.

Coach takes out his stopwatch. "Can you do 60 jumping jacks in 1 minute?" he asks his team.

"That's one jumping jack each second!"

If you were a minute, you would be part of an analog clock. The numbers on an analog clock stand for hours. The small hand marks the hour. It is called the hour hand. One hour is divided into 60 minutes. The 60 small marks on the clock stand for minutes. The big hand marks the minute. It is called the minute hand.

It is 7 o'clock!

hour hand

minute hand

When the minute hand is on the 1,
it is 5 minutes after the hour.
It is 5 minutes past 7 o'clock.

minute hand

hour hand

9

If you were a minute, you would be part of a digital clock.
A digital clock shows the hour first, then the minutes.

It's 7:25. The alarm clock is beeping.
It's time to wake up!

Cartoons start at 7:30!

If you were a minute, you could measure the amount of time it takes to get ready for school.

The school bus comes at 8 o'clock. In Spring, it takes Porter 5 minutes to get ready for school.

In fall, it takes Carlos 10 minutes to get ready for school.

In winter, it takes Flora 20 minutes to get ready for school.

If you were a minute, you could shape the school day.
You would help everyone stay on schedule.

$$3+2=5$$
$$1+6=7$$
$$4+2=6$$

math begins

math ends

Carlos learns math for 45 minutes.

lunch begins   lunch ends

Porter eats lunch for 30 minutes.

recess begins   recess ends

Flora enjoys recess for 10 minutes.

If you were a minute, you could measure the amount of time it takes to do some sports.

After school, Carlos runs five laps around the track in 15 minutes.

Flora runs five laps in 10 minutes.

It takes Porter 2 minutes to paddle across the pool.

17

If you were a minute, you could measure the amount of time it takes to travel.

After practice, it takes Flora 10 minutes to skateboard home.

It takes Carlos 12 minutes to bike home.

It takes Porter 15 minutes to ride his scooter home.

If you were a minute, you could measure the amount of time it takes to make supper.

Flora cooks a frozen pizza in 20 minutes.

Porter orders a pizza.
The pizza arrives in 30 minutes.

Carlos makes a pizza
in 60 minutes, or 1 hour.

21

You would mark the beginning
of the day and the end of the day ...

8:30

... if you were a minute.

Minute Activity: Timing Your Day

What you need:

a watch or a clock   a piece of paper   a pen or pencil

What you do:

1. Starting in the morning, make a list of each activity you do during the day. Write down as many things as you can.

2. Throughout the day, track how much time it takes you to do each activity. Round to the nearest minute. How much time does it take to brush your teeth? Comb your hair? Get dressed?

3. At the end of the day, answer the following questions:
   a. Are there any surprises on your list?
   b. Which activities take the longest amount of time?
   c. Which activities take the shortest amount of time?
   d. What do you spend most of your time doing?

4. Compare your list to a friend's list. How are your lists different? How are they alike?

23

Glossary

analog clock—a clock that has a minute hand and an hour hand

digital clock—a clock that shows information in the form of numbers

hour—a unit used to measure time; there are 60 minutes in 1 hour

minute—a unit used to measure time; there are 60 seconds in 1 minute

second—a very small unit of time; there are 60 seconds in 1 minute

To Learn More

More Books to Read

Murphy, Stuart J. *It's About Time*. New York: HarperCollins, 2005.

Scheunemann, Pam. *Time to Learn About Seconds, Minutes & Hours*. Edina, Minn.: ABDO Pub., 2008.

On the Web

FactHound offers a safe, fun way to find educator-approved Internet sites related to this book.

Here's what you do:

1. Visit *www.facthound.com*
2. Choose your grade level.
3. Begin your search.

This book's ID number is 9781404852013

Index

Look for all of the books in the Math Fun series:

If You Were a Divided-by Sign

If You Were a Fraction

If You Were a Minus Sign

If You Were a Minute

If You Were a Plus Sign

If You Were a Pound or a Kilogram

If You Were a Quart or a Liter

If You Were a Set

If You Were a Times Sign

If You Were an Even Number

If You Were an Inch or a Centimeter

If You Were an Odd Number